Gal **Gadot**

A New Kind of Action Hero

By Vanessa Oswald

Published in 2020 by
Lucent Press, an Imprint of Greenhaven Publishing, LLC
353 3rd Avenue
Suite 255
New York, NY 10010

Designer: Deanna Paternostro
Editor: Jill Keppeler

Library of Congress Cataloging-in-Publication Data

Names: Oswald, Vanessa, author.
Title: Gal Gadot : a new kind of action hero / Vanessa Oswald.
Description: New York : Lucent Press, 2020. | Series: People in the news |
    Includes bibliographical references and index.
Identifiers: LCCN 2019001476 (print) | LCCN 2019005656 (ebook) | ISBN
    9781534567788 (ebook) | ISBN 9781534567771 (pbk. book) | ISBN
    9781534567092 (library bound book)
Subjects: LCSH: Gadot, Gal, 1985– —Juvenile literature. |
    Actors—Israel—Biography—Juvenile literature.
Classification: LCC PN2919.8.G33 (ebook) | LCC PN2919.8.G33 O89 2020 (print)
    | DDC 791.4302/8092 [B]—dc23
LC record available at https://lccn.loc.gov/2019001476

Printed in the United States of America

CPSIA compliance information: Batch #BS19KL: For further information contact Greenhaven Publishing LLC, New York,
New York, at 1-844-317-7404.

Please visit our website, www.greenhavenpublishing.com. For a free color
catalog of all our high-quality books, call toll free 1-844-317-7404 or fax
1-844-317-7405.

Contents

Foreword

We live in a world where the latest news is always available and where it seems we have unlimited access to the lives of the people in the news. Entire television networks are devoted to news about politics, sports, and entertainment. Social media has allowed people to have an unprecedented level of interaction with celebrities. We have more information at our fingertips than ever before. However, how much do we really know about the people we see on television news programs, social media feeds, and magazine covers?

Despite the constant stream of news, the full stories behind the lives of some of the world's most newsworthy men and women are often unknown. Who was Gal Gadot before she became Wonder Woman? What does LeBron James do when he is not playing basketball? What inspires Lin-Manuel Miranda?

This series aims to answer questions like these about some of the biggest names in pop culture, sports, politics, and technology. While the subjects of this series come from all walks of life and areas of expertise, they share a common magnetism that has made them all captivating figures in the public eye. They have shaped the world in some unique way, and—in many cases—they are poised to continue to shape the world for many years to come.

These biographies are not just a collection of basic facts. They tell compelling stories that show how each figure grew to become a powerful public personality. Each book aims to paint a complete, realistic picture of its subject—from the challenges they overcame to the controversies they caused. In doing so, each book reinforces the idea that even the most famous faces on the news are real people who are much more complex than we are often shown in brief video clips or sound bites. Readers are also reminded that there is even more to a person than what they present to the world through social media posts, press releases, and interviews. The whole story of a person's life can only be discovered by digging beneath the surface of their public persona, and that is what this series allows readers to do.

The books in this series are filled with enlightening quotes from speeches and interviews given by the subjects, as well as quotes and anecdotes from those who know their story best: family, friends, coaches, and colleagues. All quotes are noted to provide guidance for further research. Detailed lists of additional resources are also included, as are timelines, indexes, and unique photographs. These text features come together to enhance the reading experience and encourage readers to dive deeper into the stories of these influential men and women.

Fame can be fleeting, but the subjects featured in this series have real staying power. They have fundamentally impacted their respective fields and have achieved great success through hard work and true talent. They are men and women defined by their accomplishments, and they are often seen as role models for the next generation. They have left their mark on the world in a major way, and their stories are meant to inspire readers to leave their mark, too.

A Woman Destined to Empower

Gal Gadot has become the newest person to portray one of the most well-known female comic book icons—one known to the world as Wonder Woman. Her life leading up to this moment prepared her to take on this important role, but at the same time, the opportunity was completely unexpected. When she was younger, Gadot was not exactly sure what she wanted to do with her life. She went from being a pageant contestant and a model to serving in the Israeli military. Then, she became a law student and, finally, an actress. It took her some time to find her passion.

Once Gadot began acting, her love for the art form grew. In her first major role in the *Fast and the Furious* franchise, she gained experience as an actress playing an ongoing character in multiple action films. This allowed her to create depth and develop the character. From there, she went on to star in other action films and was featured in a few comedy films as well. As time went on, Gadot went from someone who had never acted in her life to an actress who has played many kinds of roles.

Positive Role Model

While Gadot was getting started as an actress, she was asked

Gal Gadot is now one of the most recognizable people in Hollywood.

repeatedly what her dream role would be. She said, "I just want to play the real woman who's strong and confident and show the better side of women that … we see from time to time, but it's not exactly what we see all the time in movies."[1] At first, Gadot was not always cast in film roles that showed her as a strong, capable, and independent woman. After she landed the role of Wonder Woman, though, one of Gadot's main priorities became to choose roles that set good examples for her two daughters, Alma and Maya. She wants them to see her playing characters with honorable qualities that can help them navigate their own lives with the same self-assurance.

Upon getting the chance to play the latest version of Wonder Woman, Gadot said she felt like the "luckiest girl in the world."[2] She was finally playing a character who represented everything she had been looking for in her ideal role.

Wonder Woman was the first major motion picture about a female superhero. It grossed more than $800 million worldwide, surpassing the amount any other individual superhero origin movie had earned at that time. It also became the highest-grossing film ever directed by a woman at the time of its release. Gadot brought renewed popularity to the DC Extended Universe film franchise, which included seven films as of early 2019. However, more are in the works, including more starring Gadot.

Future of a Worldwide Icon

Assuming the role of the world's most iconic female superhero was a big responsibility. Many people look up to the character of Wonder Woman for her strength, intelligence, and grace; she represents female empowerment in its full capacity. Gadot wanted to make sure she was portraying the character properly—in all her glory as a very influential figure.

The actress will continue her depiction of the superhero in the upcoming film *Wonder Woman 1984* and potentially in other DC projects that have yet to be announced. However, Gadot has several other projects in progress as well. They will have her taking on new characters and bringing more versatility to her acting portfolio. With such huge success so early in her acting career, Gadot may feel pressure to top her epic performance as Wonder Woman. However, one thing is certain—she will continue exciting viewers no matter what role she plays.

Chapter **One**

Growing Up
in Israel

Gal Gadot's childhood shaped her into a strong woman with the empathy, determination, and intelligence to achieve greatness. Her parents taught her valuable life lessons she would go on to remember and use into adulthood. As a citizen of Israel, Gadot was taught commitment and appreciation for her heritage and where she came from. Even though she was uncertain about her career aspirations when she was growing up, she knew she was capable of many things, and she was prepared for whatever challenges were ahead of her.

Family Ties

Gadot was born in Petah Tikva, Israel, on April 30, 1985. Her mother, Irit, a physical education teacher, and her father, Michael, an engineer and a sixth-generation Israeli, had the last name Greenstein, but they changed it to Gadot before she was born. In Hebrew, her first name means "wave," and her last name means "riverbanks."[3] Her ancestry is also Polish, Czechoslovakian, Austrian, and German.

Gadot was raised with her younger sister, Dana, in a traditional Jewish household in the neighboring city of Rosh HaAyin. The family regularly attended temple and

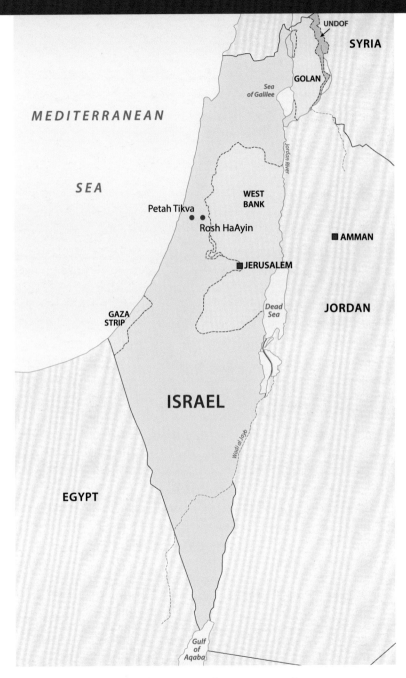

About 50,000 people live in Rosh HaAyin today.

celebrated Jewish holidays. Being Jewish is an important part of Gadot's life:

> I definitely have a strong sense of my Jewish and Israeli identity. … I was brought up in a very Jewish, Israeli family environment, so of course my heritage is very important to me. I want people to have a good impression of Israel. I don't feel like I'm an ambassador for my country, but I do talk about Israel a lot—I enjoy telling people about where I come from and my religion.[4]

Gadot's maternal grandfather was a Holocaust survivor. He was 13 when the Nazis invaded Czechoslovakia. His father lost his life while serving in the army, while the rest of their family was sent to the Auschwitz concentration camp. While his mother and brother died in the gas chambers, he made it out alive. "His entire family was murdered—it's unthinkable," Gadot said. "He affected me a lot. After all the horrors he'd seen, he was like this damaged bird, but he was always hopeful and positive and full of love. If I was raised in a place where these values were not so strong, things would be different."[5]

Active Lifestyle

As a child, Gadot lived a somewhat sheltered life. Her mother was always encouraging her to be active and discouraged her from watching TV. "My mom is amazing," Gadot told ESPN. "She taught me how to swim when I was 4. … [It was always] 'take the ball and go outside and play with the neighbors.' She always instructed us to be physical, and I think that's why I am still so connected to my body and expressing myself through it."[6] However, she does remember watching two movies that had a significant influence on her: 1987's *The Princess Bride* and 1984's *The NeverEnding Story*. In fact, her first movie crush was Atreyu, who was played by actor Noah Hathaway in the latter. "I had a thing for boys with long hair when I was nine,"[7] Gadot said with a laugh during an interview with *W* magazine.

Child actor Noah Hathaway starred in *The NeverEnding Story.*

Gadot was an outgoing, confident, and friendly child. She was also a good student and a tomboy who always had a few wounds and scratches on her knees. Gadot enjoyed other people's company, especially because she was an only child until she was eight. As a child, she had no clear aspirations to become an actress, but she did like to perform:

> *I really liked to perform. My mother always tells this story: I was five. They had a party, and they'd put me to bed. I heard everyone on the rooftop, and I went upstairs. No one paid any attention to me, so I took a hose and sprayed everyone. Very elegant, right? "It's meeeee! Look at me!" I loved the attention.*[8]

Gadot's parents taught many essential life lessons to her and her sister. They made sure their daughters knew the importance of believing in themselves and taught them never to second-guess their value in the world. In particular, her mother taught them that girls and women are strong and can pursue any career they want: "My mom raised my sister and me to be confident women with aspirations," Gadot said. "And I always felt capable. I'm not saying that I'm stronger than most men … but we all have the same brains and we can achieve the same things."[9]

As she got older, Gadot played sports, including basketball, volleyball, and tennis. In high school, she majored in biology and played on the basketball team, which she says she was good at because of her height. However, as the years went on, her true passion became dancing. For 12 years, she took classes in dance styles including ballet, hip-hop, modern, and jazz. She became so serious about dance that she even considered becoming a choreographer when she grew up.

Gadot also had a fondness for the singer Madonna. At one of her school events, she performed with a group of girls to Madonna's "Vogue."

Pageant World

Gadot had the kinds of first jobs many young people do, such as babysitting for her neighbors when she was 12 and working at Burger King when she was 15. However, every now and then, people would approach her with modeling opportunities. At first, she did not have any interest in modeling whatsoever: "I was like, 'Posing for money? Ugh, it's not for me.'"[10] At 18, she caught the attention of a talent scout who told her she should try out for the 2004 Miss Israel beauty pageant. Gadot's mother and a friend decided to enter her in the pageant. When Gadot found out she'd been chosen to compete, she decided to do it. She thought it would be a fun story to tell her future grandchildren.

During the pageant, Gadot answered interview questions and wore evening gowns. She also performed the Hebrew

Madonna (shown here) is known around the world, including in Israel.

Gadot won the title of Miss Israel when she was 19 years old.

version of Irene Cara's 1980 hit song "Fame" with the 19 other contestants. To her surprise, she won the title of Miss Israel 2004. That meant she was entered into the Miss Universe pageant. If she won the title of Miss Universe, Gadot knew she would have to move to New York City for a year. She did not want to be away from her family that long. Her heart was also not into competing in pageants; she knew she was destined for something else. "I really didn't want to win the Miss Universe pageant," Gadot said. "It was too much being Miss Israel. I was 19. I wasn't that type of girl. I rebelled."[11] To make sure she did not win the Miss Universe pageant, she showed up late to the rehearsals, wore the wrong attire, and did not put effort into answering an interview question from one of the judges, who happened to be singer and dancer Paula Abdul. "They tell you to come to breakfast in a gown," Gadot said, recalling the experience. "I was like, 'No *way* am I having breakfast in a gown!' Who needs to wear an evening gown at 10:30 a.m.?"[12]

Life as a Soldier and Student

As an Israeli citizen, Gadot was required to serve two years in the Israel Defense Forces (IDF) after high school. She served her time in the IDF starting in 2005. After enduring a grueling three-month boot camp, Gadot served as a combat instructor. Her job was to train soldiers and keep them in shape. While she learned how to use weapons in boot camp, she was never in a combat situation and never had to use a weapon in the field. Gadot has said she is proud of where she comes from and that she was happy to serve her country.

After her time in the military, Gadot went on to study law and international relations at IDC Herzliya, a college in Israel. Looking back, she realized this field of study was not the best fit for her because of her natural desire for harmony. "Honestly, it's like the worst thing I could ever have done to myself because I'm so bad when it comes to conflict," Gadot said. "I like when people get along. ... I don't want to mess with tension and fights."[13] However, she also said she can see where her interest in law came from, given the similarities

Israel Defense Forces

The Israel Defense Forces (IDF) was established in 1948 after Israel declared independence. Its mission is "to defend the existence, territorial integrity and sovereignty of the state of Israel. To protect the inhabitants of Israel and to combat all forms of terrorism which threaten the daily life."[1]

The IDF includes the ground forces, air force, and navy. These forces are known in Israel by the Hebrew acronym Tzahal. Both men and women have served in the IDF since the start, and both served before that in other defense organizations. All Israeli citizens who are Jewish and over 18 must serve in the military—two years for women and three years for men. Since 2012, there has been a steady rise in women seeking combat roles in the IDF. In 2013, there were 1,365 women entering combat roles. By 2016, this number had risen to 2,100, and then 2,700 by 2017.

1. Quoted in "Code of Ethics and Mission," Israel Defense Forces. www.idf.il/en/minisites/code-of-ethics-and-mission/.

between law and acting. This, she said, is especially true when reading verdicts, which are similar to scripts in a way and tell the story of each case.

Bond Girl Tryout

During Gadot's time studying law, a casting director from London, England, was scouring modeling and acting agencies in Israel, looking for the next Bond girl for the 2008 film *Quantum of Solace*. A Bond girl is a starring woman in a James Bond movie. The casting director happened to be at the modeling agency Gadot worked with, spied her card on the board, and asked to see her. However, Gadot had no acting experience, so she was not going to try out for the part at first. She told her agent that she was busy studying. "I'm way too serious and smart to be an actress, and besides, the script is all in English," she said she told the agent. "I spoke English, but I wasn't comfortable with it."[14] After her agent kept begging her to go to the

Castro

While Gadot was studying law and international relations at IDC Herzliya in Israel, she was also building up a portfolio for her modeling and acting careers. One of her first major modeling jobs was with the Israeli fashion brand Castro. She was the main model for the brand from 2008 to 2016.

Castro started with Aharon Castro, who was born in Thessaloniki, Greece, and came to what is now Tel Aviv, Israel, with his family in 1933. His mother, Anina, a dressmaker who graduated from the Greek School of Fashion, was a major influence on him. When they came to Israel, she started a dress salon in the family's small apartment. "In today's terms, Mom was a fashion designer, in the full sense of the word," Aharon Castro said. "She employed 15 seamstresses while she herself dealt with the design and sampling of the items."[1]

In 1948, Castro opened his first textile and fashion business in Tel Aviv. As the success of the company grew, he opened a factory in the basement below the shop. In time, Castro began selling his clothes to luxury department stores, then exporting his clothing to European stores. Aharon Castro died in 2017, but his family still runs the company.

1. Quoted in "The Development of the Castro Fashion House," Castro.com. www.castro.com/en/development_of_castro.

audition, Gadot finally decided to try. She remembers trying to study the two scenes she was supposed to read at the audition while driving at the same time.

When Gadot arrived at the audition, she was honest with the casting director. She admitted that she was not an actress and only went there because her agent insisted it was a good idea. Gadot said she would understand if the director did not want to hear her read the script because of that. Gadot's outright honesty was refreshing to the casting director, which made her even more intrigued to see Gadot's audition. Gadot read a few sections of the script and, as she had predicted, did not get chosen for the part. The role of Camille Montes ultimately went to Ukranian-born French actress Olga Kurylenko.

Actress Olga Kurylenko (center) was given the part of Camille Montes in *Quantum of Solace* over Gal Gadot.

However, with this audition, Gadot had realized that acting was fun. She started working with an acting coach. "I was like, 'Wow, this is fascinating—this is so much more exciting than going to … law school,'"[15] she said. Although she did not get the Bond movie part, she began receiving callbacks for other roles. However, she still failed to land the parts. Finally, in 2007, Gadot landed her first acting role on the Israeli TV series *Bubot*, which translates to "Babes" in English. She played Miriam "Merry" Elkayam. When she was offered the role, she decided to stop working toward her law degree. *Bubot* ran for only one season, from 2007 to 2008. Soon after this, however, the same casting director who had pursued Gadot for the *Quantum of Solace* role encouraged her to try out for a role in the 2009 film *Fast & Furious*. She got the part, which was her first English-speaking role in a movie.

Unknown Territory

Gadot had landed a role in a major motion picture, but she had never been featured in an English-language film or television show before. This was all new to her, and she was unsure of what to expect. However, she was intrigued and excited to land the part. She had no idea how her life was about to change.

As with everything in her life, Gadot went into this new opportunity curious and open-minded. However, she had decided she would not let anyone take advantage of her. She would go on to take only roles she was comfortable with, roles that showcased women as strong and dignified individuals.

Taking the role in *Fast & Furious* meant Gadot would have to spend time in the United States away from her family in Israel, which was a tough sacrifice for her. However, this role would lead to several others and solidify her standing as a popular actress, and she was ready for the challenge.

Chapter **Two**

Speeding Toward Stardom

In 2008, Gadot was embarking on two new journeys in her life at the same time: movie acting and marriage. That was the year she married Israeli real estate developer Yaron Varsano. Her husband supported her acting aspirations and encouraged her every step of the way.

As Gadot continued working with an acting coach, she gained more experience, and her acting became increasingly more believable and captivating to audiences. She went on to play several different roles in the following years, most of them small. However, with each role, she further honed her acting skills and worked her way up to taking on an iconic movie role she never dreamed she would be playing.

Meeting Her Husband

Gadot first met Yaron Varsano in 2006, while she was serving in the IDF. They met through mutual friends at a "very strange party," in the Israeli desert, of which Gadot said, "It was all about yoga, chakras, and eating healthy—we didn't exactly find ourselves there, but we found each other."[16] She said it was like love at first sight when they met—but that she was "too young to get it."[17] Varsano, who is 10 years older than Gadot, knew instantly that he wanted to marry her. On

Gadot met her husband, Yaron Varsano, during her time in the Israel Defense Forces.

their second date, he told her that he was serious and that he would not wait more than two years to ask her to marry him.

The couple married on September 28, 2008, and had their first child, their daughter Alma, in 2011. Gadot contemplated whether she should continue acting while she had a family. She felt guilty traveling so much with a young child and her husband and felt like she was dragging them with her to auditions. Gadot spoke about how her husband eased her anxiety about pursuing her dreams while also having a family:

> When Alma was around two, I was really anxious about how to travel with a child, moving her from one country to the other, all the different languages. It was my husband who told me: "Gal, think about what kind of a role model you want to be. If you want to show Alma that she can follow her dreams, that's what you should do, and we will figure out the logistics."[18]

With Varsano's support and encouragement, Gadot was able to realize that, while her family was her first priority, she did not have to sacrifice her dreams of acting just because she was married and had a child. With this renewed confidence, she took Hollywood by storm and landed her first ongoing role in a film franchise.

Gisele Yashar

Gadot's first big break was as Gisele Yashar in the *Fast and the Furious* film franchise. This series of suspenseful action movies is about the world of illegal street racing. The films mainly take place in Los Angeles, California, but also have elements in other parts of the world, such as Brazil; London, England; and Tokyo, Japan. The two main characters in most of the movies are ex-convict and well-known street racer Dominic "Dom" Toretto, played by Vin Diesel, and undercover police officer Brian O'Conner, who was played by Paul Walker.

Gadot made her first appearance in the franchise's fourth film, 2009's *Fast & Furious*. In this film, Gisele is a liaison for Mexican drug lord Arturo Braga, who was played by John Ortiz. Dom winds up saving Gisele's life, and she helps him.

In the fifth film in the franchise, *Fast Five*, Gisele made another appearance, joining Dom's team as a weapons expert after she is revealed to be an ex-Mossad agent. Mossad, similar to the CIA, is the national intelligence agency of Israel. This detail of Gadot's character related to her real-life experience as a combat instructor in the IDF, which allowed her to draw from those personal experiences to inspire the character's actions in the movie.

Part of the Action

Gadot's character Gisele returned in 2013's *Fast & Furious 6*. She and others are recruited by Dom and Brian to help them prevent a heist that could kill millions of people. However, her character dies in the movie.

In this film, Gadot asked director Justin Lin if she could participate in more of the action stunts, since she did not get to do many of them in the previous two movies. "I always told Justin ... 'I want to be a tough girl. I want to do, like, all kinds of action. I want to have gunshots. I want to fly up [in] the air on the motorcycle. ... I want to do it all by myself."[19] He agreed to let her have more action scenes in the sixth film, although he did ask if she wanted a stunt double. Gadot refused one and said she was more than capable of performing all her own stunts.

Speaking about the qualities of her character in the *Fast and the Furious* movies, Gadot said,

> *I'm very proud of her. I think she's an amazing role model. She's very strong, but she lets herself be soft and be happy and be feminine at the same time. She's very clever ... sophisticated ... smart. She can see like a few steps ahead. She's one of the boys, which I always love. I mean it's so nice*

Gadot and her costars attended the *Fast & Furious 6* premiere at the Empire, Leicester Square, on May 7, 2013, in London.

> *and cool ... not to be a poshy girl, but to be one of the guys. She's very down to earth and all she cares about is important stuff, like love [and] independence.*[20]

The *Fast and Furious* journey had ended for Gadot, but a tragic event during the filming of *Furious 7* shocked her and the rest of her castmates. One of the main actors in the franchise died in a car accident. This news affected all the actors and crew members who had been affiliated with the franchise's many films.

Death of a Friend

On November 30, 2013, in Valencia, Santa Clarita, California, Paul Walker, who starred in most of the *Fast and the Furious* films, died in a car crash. While he played a

Paul Walker

Paul William Walker IV was born on September 12, 1973, in Glendale, California. At a young age, he began modeling and was interested in acting. His first venture into acting was the 1986 horror comedy *Monster in the Closet*. Over the years, he appeared in many movies, including *She's All That* and *Varsity Blues*.

In 2001, Walker finally made his big break when he was cast in *The Fast and the Furious* as police officer Brian O'Conner. He appeared in six of the eight movies in the *Fast and the Furious* film franchise.

In 2013, Walker died in a car crash. He was mourned by many, including his *Fast and Furious* costars.

Paul Walker starred in his first movie in 1986, when he was 13 years old.

street racer on screen, Walker was also a racing enthusiast in real life. His grandfather had been the first man to break 160 miles (258 km) per hour with the Ford Falcon in the 1960s.

At the time of his death, Walker was filming *Furious 7*. When the news of his death broke, all the actors on the set were devastated by the loss of their friend. As it came time to release the seventh film in the franchise, the project became a way to pay homage to Walker. "This was a labor of love," Diesel said. "It was in some ways the hardest film I ever had to do because the relationships that you see onscreen are so real. When the tragedy happened, I lost my best friend, I lost my brother."[21]

Gadot was not on set at the time of Walker's death, but she felt the same sadness when she heard the news. "I loved Paul and I adored him from the very first moment that I met him because he was so grounded and down-to-earth and like the cutest, coolest dude, and so real as well,"[22] Gadot said. Gadot and Walker were not in touch between projects, as she lived in Israel, and she assumed she would see him when the next film in the franchise was released. "For me I still don't realize that he died because if there was going to be another movie some part of me thinks that I'm going to see Paul because that's just the way it is for me," Gadot said. "But it's super ... tragic."[23]

TV Appearances

After landing the role of Gisele in the *Fast and the Furious* franchise, Gadot was also chosen for guest roles on various TV series. She appeared in one episode of *Entourage*, which followed film star Vincent Chase, played by Adrian Grenier, and his close circle of friends. Gadot played the role of Lisa in a cameo in 2009.

Gadot was also featured on *The Beautiful Life: TBL*, a show about a group of male and female models who share a residence in New York City. Gadot played the role of Olivia, a model who previously dated model Cole Shepherd, played by

Gadot attended the CW and *Harper's Bazaar* launch of *The Beautiful Life: TBL* on September 12, 2009, in New York City.

Nico Tortorella. She appeared in three episodes. *The Beautiful Life: TBL* received mixed reviews from critics and ran for only one season, from September to December 2009.

In 2011, Gadot returned to another Israeli TV series, *Asfur*, which means "bird" in Arabic. The series followed four friends living in abandoned buses on a property worth millions in Jerusalem's industrial zone. The friends are forced to pay back a huge debt or else the land will be sold to the highest bidder. Gadot played the role of Kika, appearing in 17 episodes in the second season of the show.

Gadot was also featured on the Israeli TV miniseries *Kathmandu*. She played the role of Yamit Bareli in 11 episodes of the show, which was about a young couple that volunteers to establish a Chabad house—a Jewish community center—in Kathmandu, Nepal, for Israeli backpackers. This show ran for one season from May to August 2012.

Film Roles

In 2010, Gadot began landing parts in other films, such as *Date Night* and *Knight and Day*. In *Date Night*, she played Natanya, an Israeli woman dating Mark Wahlberg's character, Holbrooke Grant. The movie, which starred Steve Carell and Tina Fey, premiered in April 2010. In June 2010, Gadot appeared in *Knight and Day*, which starred Tom Cruise and Cameron Diaz. She played Naomi.

As Gadot took on different roles, she learned how to transform into people who were much different from her. While her acting skills were improving, she was waiting to land a leading role in which she could showcase all the skills she had learned. She was sometimes criticized for playing roles that lacked substance—however, one call would soon change that perception in many ways.

Even though Gadot had parts in several projects, most of the roles were small. She felt guilty about pursuing acting while commuting with her husband and daughter from Israel to Hollywood for every audition. She had come close to landing prominent roles in movies, but the rejection for those roles was becoming overwhelming as well. However, that was about to change.

In 2013, right when Gadot was ready to give up her dream and go back to Israel, she got a call from Warner Bros. studios, asking her to audition for a secret project. She read a script for director Zack Snyder and then flew back to Israel, waiting to hear if she won the part.

Chapter **Three**

Becoming
Wonder Woman

Even though Gadot never planned to become an actress, she had discovered her talent for the art form. She had evolved from a dancer to a model to an aspiring law student to an actress. She had yet to acquire the monumental role she would become known for. She was ready to get on a plane back to Israel to call it quits—and then one audition changed everything.

Life-Changing Audition

When Gadot's agent contacted her about the audition for this secret role, she had only one more week left in Los Angeles. After this week, she planned to return to Israel and give up on her dream of acting in Hollywood for the time being. She did not plan to return to the United States for a long time.

For the audition, Gadot had a scene to read in front of director Zack Snyder and casting director Lora Kennedy. According to Gadot, she thought the audition went well. Gadot and Snyder immediately hit it off; they both have families and showed each other photos of their kids. Once the audition was over, Gadot returned to Israel to shoot a movie.

However, a few weeks later, her agent called to let her know Snyder and Kennedy wanted her to do a camera test with Ben Affleck for this secret project.

She now knew it was for *Batman v Superman: Dawn of Justice*. However, she still did not know which part she was reading for. She thought that perhaps the part was Catwoman, since she would be reading with Affleck, who was playing Batman in the film.

Two days later, Snyder called Gadot to tell her the role she was auditioning for was Wonder Woman. He asked her if she knew who the character was. Gadot was not usually a fan of comic books, but she absolutely knew who Wonder Woman was.

"I don't have a clear moment where I'm like ... Wonder Woman," she said. "It's something that I was always aware of. It's like Superman; it's like a household name. Everyone knows about them and what it means. ... I knew of her, I didn't know much about her."[24]

Even though Gadot was not personally invested in the character of Wonder Woman growing up, she was invested in everything that Wonder Woman represented. She explained how she felt about auditioning for the role: "There's so many general meetings with writers and producers and directors. They always ask you the same question: What is your dream role?"[25] For her, that role was a woman who is strong, confident, and independent and who represents female empowerment in its truest sense. She realized this audition was a huge opportunity for her as an actress to play that dream role.

After flying into London from Israel, Gadot was fighting jet lag, but she was excited for the audition. When she showed up for the camera test, she saw several trailers and knew that in each trailer was another actress competing for the same role.

Director Zack Snyder (far left) and Gadot instantly got along when they met and bonded over their children.

After Gadot arrived, she was supposed to stay in her trailer until someone came to get her. She waited for several hours and started becoming stressed and anxious. After some time, Victoria Down (who later became Gadot's makeup artist for *Batman v Superman*) came into Gadot's trailer and gave her a massage with peppermint oil. Down told Gadot, "I have a good feeling about you … Let's try to wake up."[26]

Then, Gadot called her husband, who tried to help ease her anxiety. He said, "Just play some music, just dance. Do what you like to do best."[27] Gadot agreed, so she turned on Beyoncé's song "Diva" and danced around her trailer. Once the song was over, there was finally a knock on her door. It was time for the audition.

Receiving the Call

After the audition, Gadot returned to Israel. She felt good about her performance in the audition. However, she was still unsure if she would get the role. After a few weeks of no news, she began doubting herself. There had been many auditions just like this, in which she felt she had done a good job but did not get the part.

A few weeks later, Gadot was on an airplane that had just landed at the Los Angeles International Airport, which she was flying into for a different job. Gadot was still in her seat when she checked her phone and noticed she had several missed calls from her agent.

She called her agent back. Eventually, several people involved in the movie came on the line. They told her: "Gal, you are Wonder Woman."[28]

Reacting to the good news, Gadot began shouting joyously on the airplane. Many people around her gave her inquisitive looks. However, she could not tell anyone that she had the part because there had been no official statement released yet. The casting news was not released until early December 2013.

Gadot said that when she got the part, she thought back to the times she was questioned on her ideal role. "I land *Wonder Woman* and for me it was like, 'Oh my God, that was my dream role!' Only afterwards I realized that was exactly what I was talking about."[29] She was ready to take on the role and prove she was capable of portraying Diana Prince—otherwise known as Wonder Woman.

Creators of Wonder Woman

Maxwell Charles Gaines, a former elementary school principal, founded All-American Publications. He is considered to be a pioneer in the world of modern-day comic books. However, the *Chicago Daily News* at the time labeled comics a "national disgrace."[1] The literary editor of the paper suggested parents and teachers ban all comics from their children "unless we want a coming generation even more ferocious than the present one."[2] Eventually, Gaines hired psychologist and writer William Moulton Marston, known by his pen name Charles Moulton, to help defend Gaines against critics.

Since many of the complaints about comic books had to do with the violence of men, Marston had the idea to create a female superhero to counteract what he called "blood-curdling masculinity."[3] This led to the creation of Wonder Woman. The character made her debut in *All-Star Comics No. 8* at the end of 1941 and appeared on the cover of a new comic book, *Sensation Comics No. 1*, in early 1942. All-American Publications later merged with DC comics, which was created in 1934 and originally called National Allied Publications.

While Marston wrote the story, artist Harry G. Peter, generally cited as H. G. Peter, created the first drawings of Wonder Woman.

1. Quoted in Jill Lepore, "The Surprising Origin Story of Wonder Woman," *Smithsonian Magazine*, October 2014. www.smithsonianmag.com/arts-culture/origin-story-wonder-woman-180952710/.

2. Quoted in Lepore, "The Surprising Origin Story of Wonder Woman."

3. Quoted in Lepore, "The Surprising Origin Story of Wonder Woman."

William Moulton Marston created Wonder Woman in 1941. The character has gone through many changes, but some things remain the same.

Finding Wonder Woman

Snyder said he had to interview hundreds of hopeful actresses for the role of Wonder Woman. It was an exhausting process before he picked six actresses for the final test. He finally decided on Gadot, he said, because "she's strong, beautiful, and she's a kind person, which is interesting, but fierce at the same time. It's that combination of being fierce but kind at the same time that we were looking for. She can get serious, but she's amazingly fun to be around."[30]

Snyder was thrilled to welcome the character of Wonder Woman to the DC Extended Universe (DCEU) film franchise, which at that time had only released the Superman film *Man of Steel* in June 2013. He said he was shocked someone had not brought Wonder Woman to the big screen sooner.

"We haven't had a female superhero of that magnitude, and it's an amazing opportunity for the world to get behind an amazing, powerful female character," Snyder said. "I'm happy that we have the opportunity to do that. Half of my movies have female leads … maybe that's because I have so many strong women in my life."[31]

After Gadot discovered she would be playing Wonder Woman, she had a few conversations with Snyder about her character. However, she did not get a script for quite some time after she was chosen for the role.

In the meantime, she began her research on the legendary superhero. Gadot went from someone who had never read a comic book to someone who was reading every comic book she could get her hands on. She also read several other books about Wonder Woman:

> I tried to figure out her origin and … what drives her and what motivates her and who she is …Because there's so much material about Wonder Woman … you gotta decide what's relevant and what's not. So I think that the main thing for me was … she's gotta be strong and independent and powerful, obviously, but she needs to have some warmth and she needs

to be a little witty … to make her more relatable. I wanted her to be charming in a way.[32]

Intense Training

Gadot went through intense training to get ready for her Wonder Woman role. While she had been a combat instructor in the IDF and was familiar with this type of training, preparing for playing Wonder Woman was even more grueling.

She trained six to seven hours every day for six months. Her favorite part of her workout routine was the weapons training. "I know how to use a gun and I know about combat training,"[33] Gadot said. She also enjoyed learning the intricate fight choreography. "I was a dancer for 12 years and so learning the fight choreography reminded me a lot of dancing,"[34] she said.

Her workout regimen also included kung fu, kickboxing, jujitsu, swordplay, and horseback riding. "I … thought I was going to love horse riding because it always looked as if it'd be so easy," Gadot said. "It's not. It was super painful and I had tons of bruises."[35] By the end of her training, she had gained 14 pounds (6.35 kg) of muscle.

While Gadot participated in strenuous workouts, she also made sure to drink lots of water daily and maintained a healthy diet of nutritious foods, including plenty of fruits and vegetables. "I'm a foodie and I love to experience food, but at the same time I look at food as fuel and I want to give the best to my body,"[36] she said. However, when she was filming, she did not restrict herself from her favorite foods, such as burgers and ice cream. She just made sure those foods were balanced with healthy foods.

Other Film Projects

While she was preparing to play Wonder Woman, Gadot also took on other projects. In July 2014, Gadot went back to Israel and starred in her first Israeli film, titled *Kicking Out Shoshana*.

Marvel vs. DC Comics

Many people think there is a rivalry between Marvel Comics and DC Comics, the two main comics publishing companies. Both companies have developed many different storylines and characters. Both companies have also adapted those stories and characters into their own current universe of films, including the Marvel Cinematic Universe (MCU) and DCEU.

Kevin Feige, who has been president of Marvel Studios since 2007, said he does not think there is an actual rivalry between Marvel and DC Comics:

Neal Adams is a comic book artist for DC Comics. However, he has worked for Marvel as well.

There's not really a rivalry. The rivalry is much more amongst the press, I think. Geoff Johns [the current chief creative officer of DC Comics] is a very good friend of mine. We grew up together in the business and recently celebrated Richard Donner [who directed the first modern Superman film starring Christopher Reeve], who we both used to work for. So, I applaud all the success he's had. I really just look at it as a fan. When the movies perform well and are well received, it's good for us—which is why I'm always rooting for them.[1]

1. Quoted in Brian Cronin, "Marvel Vs. DC: A History of Comics' Greatest Rivalry," CBR.com, June 18, 2017. www.cbr.com/marvel-dc-rivalry-history/.

Stan Lee was a comic book writer, editor, and publisher from the 1940s to the 2010s. He died on November 12, 2018.

The film, set in Jerusalem, follows the main character Ami Shushan, played by Oshri Cohen, who is a forward for the Bnei Yerushalayim soccer team. Gadot played Mirit Ben Harush, the girlfriend of a mob boss.

In 2016, Gadot starred in several films, including the crime thriller *Triple 9*, the action crime drama *Criminal*, and the action comedy *Keeping Up with the Joneses*. *Triple 9*

Gadot attended the premiere of *Keeping Up with the Joneses* on October 8, 2016, in Los Angeles.

is about a gang of criminals and crooked police officers who plan the murder of a police officer in order to carry out a heist in Atlanta, Georgia. Gadot played the role of Elena Vlaslov. In *Criminal*, Gadot played the role of Jill Pope, the wife of Bill Pope, played by Ryan Reynolds, who is a CIA operative who dies and has his memories, secrets, and skills implanted into death-row inmate Jerico Stewart, played by Kevin Costner. In *Keeping Up with the Joneses*, Gadot played Natalie Jones, the wife of Tim Jones, played by Jon Hamm. The couple moves across the street from Jeff and Karen Gaffney, played by Zach Galifianakis and Isla Fisher, who suspect their new neighbors are secret agents.

Batman v Superman: Dawn of Justice

While Gadot starred in several films in 2016, the most important film of all was *Batman v Superman: Dawn of Justice*. In this movie, she made her debut as Wonder Woman.

Back in December 2013, when Gadot signed on to play the character of Wonder Woman, she agreed to star in three films: *Batman v Superman: Dawn of Justice* in March 2016, *Wonder Woman* in June 2017, and *Justice League* in November 2017. They are all part of the DCEU.

Gadot's appearance as Wonder Woman in *Batman v Superman: Dawn of Justice*, directed by Zack Snyder, was the first time Wonder Woman was featured in a major motion picture, even though the character had made her comic book debut more than 70 years ago and her first TV appearance more than 40 years ago (when Lynda Carter played the role of Wonder Woman). Gadot starred alongside Affleck, Henry Cavill, and Amy Adams, who played Batman, Superman, and Lois Lane, respectively.

The standalone film *Wonder Woman* was released in theaters a year after *Batman v Superman*, so audiences did not get the full story of Wonder Woman in 2016. "When you look at [*Batman v Superman*], it's a snapshot," said Patty Jenkins, director of *Wonder Woman*. "You're not getting a lot of information about her point of view."[37]

Gadot attended the premiere of *Batman v Superman: Dawn of Justice* with her costars on March 20, 2016, in New York City.

Becoming Wonder Woman **45**

Wonder Woman is first introduced in *Batman v Superman* when the supervillain Doomsday is about to crush Batman. Doomsday fails because Wonder Woman shields Batman from being harmed. Superman enters the scene, and all three superheroes work together to defeat Doomsday. Gadot described the importance of Wonder Woman's portrayal in *Batman v Superman* to *Glamour* magazine:

> *For [Batman v Superman] it was important for me that we show how independent she is. She is not relying on a man, and she's not there because of a love story. She's not there to serve someone else... She has so many strengths and powers, but at the end of the day she's a woman with a lot of emotional intelligence. She's loving... And it's all her heart—that's her strength. I think women are amazing for being able to show what they feel. I admire women who do. I think it's a mistake when women cover their emotions to look tough. I say let's own who we are and use it as a strength.* [38]

While Wonder Woman's main motivations are to promote peace, love, compassion, truth, justice, and equality, Gadot portrayed the character as still enjoying the battle. In the scene where Wonder Woman is fighting Doomsday, the supervillain knocks her down and her sword flies out of her hand. Gathering herself, Wonder Woman flashes a quick smirk, grabs her sword, and jumps right back into the battle. After they filmed this scene, Snyder asked Gadot why she smirked. She responded, "'If he's gonna mess with her, then she's gonna mess with him. And she knows she's gonna win.' At the end of the day Wonder Woman is a peace seeker. But when fight arrives, she can fight. She's a warrior and she enjoys the adrenaline of the fight." [39]

After the release of *Batman v Superman*, many critics had unfavorable reviews of the film. The *New York Times* wrote that the film "is less a free-standing film than the opening argument in a very long trial." [40] Another reviewer from Common

Sense Media wrote, "With charismatic performances and epic battle scenes, this unrelentingly serious start to a new DC Universe franchise is intriguing but also humorless and overdone." However, Gadot's performance as Wonder Woman was often praised. The Common Sense Media reviewer also wrote, "The former Israeli combat instructor has what it takes."[41]

After making her debut as Wonder Woman in *Batman v Superman*, Gadot began gearing up to star in her own stand-alone movie, *Wonder Woman*, which takes place—for the most part—long before the events of *Batman v Superman*. Wonder Woman's appearance in *Batman v Superman* was so brief audiences did not really get to know the intricacies of her character. In *Wonder Woman*, they were introduced to Diana's backstory, the qualities she stands for, and the battles she is willing to fight to save mankind.

Chapter **Four**

A Female Hero

Gadot was preparing for her biggest film yet—one that would solidify her career as an established and well-rounded Hollywood actress. She began filming *Wonder Woman* in May 2015. Sometimes she would bring her daughter Alma, who was five years old at the time, to the set with her. Alma would see her mother dressed up as Wonder Woman and ask, "Mummy, if you wear a tiara does that mean you're a queen and then I'm a princess?" Gadot responded, "Well, I'm playing dress up, this is dress up."[42]

While Alma was a fan of princesses, she also observed that most stories involving princesses hardly ever feature the princess as the hero. Gadot remembered reading Alma a story one time and her daughter said, "The prince is always so brave and courageous and strong."[43] Gadot then asked her what she thought of the princess, and Alma said, "They always fall asleep and then the prince is the one to wake them up. And they do nothing."[44] Alma's remark showed how underrepresented female heroes can be in children's stories, but Gadot knew she would soon be playing a strong female superhero and she would serve as a role model for her daughter and other girls.

Coming of Age

The opening scene of *Wonder Woman* connects the film to *Batman v Superman*. Men from Wayne Enterprises, the company owned by Bruce Wayne (otherwise known as Batman), are shown delivering a briefcase to Diana, who is working as a curator of antiques at the Louvre Museum in Paris, France. Inside the briefcase is a photo of Diana with Steve Trevor, played by Chris Pine, and the other men she battled alongside during World War I. A note is included, referring to the photo, that reads, "I found the original. Maybe one day you'll tell me your story."[45] This leads Diana to think back to her childhood and her coming of age when she first became Wonder Woman.

Gadot explained the differences between her character in *Batman v Superman* and in *Wonder Woman*: "The character that we shot, that I played in [*Batman v Superman*] was more realistic and more mature and more of a woman. In this one, this is the coming of age of Diana. She starts as a very … naive, positive, happy, seeking-for-good girl, but in [*Batman v Superman*], … she's been through a lot. She already understood the complexity of human beings."[46]

As a child, Diana is rambunctious and headstrong. She wants to learn how to fight like the other Amazons, the legendary race of female warriors who live on Themyscira, an island given to them by the gods. However, her mother, Hippolyta (played by actress Connie Nielsen), queen of the Amazons, forbids it because she wants to protect Diana. Diana's aunt Antiope (played by actress Robin Wright—whose other most famous movie role may be as the title character in 1987's *The Princess Bride*), the military general of the Amazons, starts to train Diana in secret. The scenes in the film set on Themyscira were praised by many because they featured numerous powerful female characters who existed independent of male influence. Many women felt empowered seeing so many strong female warriors in one film.

The Origin Story

Marston created Wonder Woman in 1941, but her origin story has changed over the years. Originally, Wonder Woman was known as Princess Diana, daughter of Hippolyta, queen of the Amazons, who molded her out of clay. Then, Aphrodite, the goddess of love, breathed life into her, leaving her without a male father. In other versions, the origin story has been changed, with Hippolyta and Zeus, the ruler of the Greek gods, as her biological parents. However, a few key elements of Diana's story often remain the same.

Over the years, the Wonder Woman character in comics has endured many physical transformations and changing storylines, some interesting and others strange. In the 1940s, she started out as a feminist icon. In the 1950s, her stories became more focused on marriage and modeling. She even surrendered her powers in the 1960s so she could be closer to Steve. In the 1970s, the character became a feminist symbol again and was featured on the first cover of Gloria Steinem's *Ms.* magazine.

From 1975 to 1979, the character got her own live-action TV series, titled *Wonder Woman* and starring Lynda Carter. In the 1980s, George Perez took over writing Wonder Woman for the comics. He gave her the ability to fly and made her as strong as Superman.

At one point in the 1990s, Wonder Woman in the comics took a job at a taco restaurant after she was presumed dead following an adventure in space. In the 2000s, Wonder Woman became more of a political figure and entered the business world.

Lynda Carter became famous as TV's Wonder Woman in the 1970s.

In one scene in the film, Diana is older and participating in intense battle training and is sword fighting with Antiope. After knocking a sword out of Antiope's hands, she looks away from the fighting for a second and Antiope pushes her, knocking her to the ground. Antiope says, "Never let your guard down. You expect a battle to be fair. A battle will never be fair."[47] However, as Antiope swings her sword at Diana, the princess crosses her arms in front of her face—and, suddenly, a jolt of power emanates from her, sending Antiope flying across the field. This is when Diana first realizes she may be special, although she does not know the full extent of her powers. Soon after that, she sees a plane crash into the sea. She immediately dives into the ocean to rescue the pilot—Steve Trevor.

Steve Trevor and Man's World

Steve Trevor, played by Chris Pine in the movie, has been a DC comics character as long as Wonder Woman has. He has been her love interest, friend, and partner (and a few times, her husband) in many different versions of both characters. In many versions, Trevor, a pilot, crashes on Themyscira and Diana saves him. Then she returns with him to "Man's World," although the reason why varies.

In the movie, Steve is a pilot and a spy with the American Expeditionary Forces assigned to British Intelligence. He needs to return to Great Britain with information on secret weapons and plans that could end World War I. The Amazons know nothing about the war. Diana believes it is the work of Ares, god of war, and she wishes to leave with Steve to find and conquer the god. Her mother forbids her from going, but she sneaks out at night, taking a sword, shield, and the Lasso of Truth.

Diana later explains to her mother her desire to help humankind, and her words were inspirational for many viewers: "I cannot stand by while innocent lives are lost. If no one else will defend the world from Ares, then I must … I'm willing to fight for those that cannot fight for themselves."[48] Her mother tells her if she leaves that she may never return, and Diana answers, "Who will I be if I stay?"[49]

Gadot and Pine worked closely together in the movie *Wonder Woman*.

Facing Scrutiny

The reviews of *Wonder Woman* varied; some critics loved the movie, but others offered up sexist remarks. David Edelstein of *Vulture* opened his review commenting mostly on Gadot's appearance and almost completely neglected to mention her acting abilities: "The only grace note in the generally clunky *Wonder Woman* is its star, the five-foot-ten-inch Israeli actress and model Gal Gadot, who is somehow the perfect blend of superbabe-in-the-woods innocence and mouthiness."[1]

In Leigh Paatsch's review for the *Herald Sun*, he called *Wonder Woman* an "empty-calorie entree before the main course of DC's all-star *Justice League*," and wrote, "Perhaps you shouldn't send a Gal to do a Woman's work,"[2] referring to Gadot's appearance again, hinting that she is too small physically to play the role of Wonder Woman. Paatsch also overly praised Chris Pine's role: "Luckily, the day is continually saved by a lively, hardworking Chris Pine as Wonder Woman's wisecracking second banana and occasional love interest. Without him, it wouldn't just be a long movie. It would be a long dull movie."[3]

A.O. Scott of the *New York Times* wrote a favorable review of the movie. He not only mentioned Gadot's acting skills but also refrained from critiquing her body image: "It cleverly combines genre elements into something reasonably fresh, touching and fun ... Ms. Gadot ... has a regal, effortlessly charismatic screen presence."[4]

Paul Asay of Pluggedin.com made many positive remarks about the film. He noted that a standalone female superhero film was way overdue, and he said that Gadot did not disappoint in this role. Asay was also impressed with how accurate Gadot's portrayal of the original character was:

> *Wonder Woman is a departure from DC's recent template in that she's not really a grim, edgy departure at all. She stays true to the emotional roots of the character. Moreover, she stands for something: She believes. She inspires. In an entertainment landscape obsessed with flawed heroes, unlikeable heroes and antiheroes, Diana is— unapologetically—a real hero. Full stop. How delightfully refreshing.*[5]

Wonder Woman earned Gadot many new fans, especially new female fans who were inspired by her performance.

Gadot herself was beyond grateful to portray Wonder Woman: "This character is so big and iconic, and the expectations that all of the fans have for it are huge. I feel very privileged that I got the opportunity to portray such an iconic, strong female character. I adore this character and everything that she stands for—love, compassion, acceptance and truth."[6]

1. David Edelstein, "*Wonder Woman* Is a Star Turn for Gal Gadot, But the Rest Is Pretty Clunky," *Vulture*, June 1, 2017. www.vulture.com/2017/06/movie-review-wonder-woman-is-a-star-turn-for-gal-gadot.html.

2. Leigh Paatsch, "Gal Gadot's Wonder Woman Is the Best DC Comics Movie Yet But That's Not Saying Much," *Herald Sun*, May 31, 2017. www.heraldsun.com.au/entertainment/movies/leigh-paatsch/gal-gadots-wonder-woman-is-the-best-dc-comics-movie-yet-but-thats-not-saying-much/news-story/08e726f81e5827ba595b5 08031b8c5d9.

3. Paatsch, "Gal Gadot's Wonder Woman Is the Best DC Comics Movie Yet But That's Not Saying Much."

4. A.O. Scott, "Review: 'Wonder Woman' Is a Blockbuster That Lets Itself Have Fun," *New York Times*, May 31, 2017. www.nytimes.com/2017/05/31/movies/wonder-woman-review-gal-gadot.html?referrer=google_kp.

5. Paul Asay, "Movie Review: Wonder Woman," Pluggedin.com, accessed on December 27, 2018. www.pluggedin.com/movie-reviews/wonder-woman-2017/.

6. Quoted in Mia McNiece, "Gal Gadot Felt 'Privileged' to Play Wonder Woman: 'I Adore This Character,'" *Entertainment Weekly*, May 31, 2017. ew.com/movies/2017/05/31/gal-gadot-chris-pine-wonder-woman/.

In many of the scenes in *Wonder Woman*, Diana displays her strength and independence in several ways. She is not dependent on a man; most of the time the men are dependent on her. She inspires all her own actions and is not influenced by men, or other women, telling her what to do.

For example, as Diana and Steve are traveling, she tells him that once she defeats Ares the war will end and things will be better. He says he appreciates her spirit but that there is not a lot they can do—but if they return to London, they can find the men who can. Diana says, "I'm the man who can."[50] She sees no reason she should have to depend on men to do anything.

The theme of Diana being strong and in control continues when they get to London. There, Steve tries to protect Diana when they are attacked, but she blocks the bullets and protects him. She does most of the fighting in this scene, while Steve gets one punch in at the end.

When Diana and Steve bring the information to a council in London, all the men are shocked by Diana's presence. One man scolds Steve for bringing her there, and he has to introduce her as his secretary. Diana is then shocked and horrified when the leaders tell Steve to do nothing to stop the development and possible use of a new weapon by the enemy. "I am not with you," she tells them. "You would knowingly sacrifice all those lives, as if they mean less than yours! As if they mean nothing? Where I come from, generals don't hide in their offices like cowards. They fight alongside their soldiers. They die with them on the battlefield. You should be ashamed."[51] This scene and many others showcased Gadot's ability to portray Diana's righteous anger over the way humans wage war.

Saving Lives

After the scenes in London, Diana and Steve, with a handful of Steve's comrades, head for the battlefield anyway. Diana wants to try to save everyone, but Steve tells her she cannot possibly do so. Eventually, however, Diana takes the chance to try to save a town taken by the Germans. This leads to one of the movie's most iconic moments, in which Diana storms the battlefield's "No Man's Land" in her Wonder Woman attire, blocking bullets with her wrist cuffs and shield.

For many viewers, the No Man's Land scene was one of the best superhero movie moments ever. The men around Diana tell her that she cannot do anything to help and to stay safely out of No Man's Land. They tell her that saving the town is impossible. Still, Diana—in her full Amazon armor—ignores them. She crosses into No Man's Land in classic movie slow motion and charges forward—a true female hero in action.

Gadot is seen here posing for photos at the *Wonder Woman* premiere with, from left, Connie Nielsen, Danny Huston, Chris Pine, Patty Jenkins, Elena Anaya, Robin Wright, and Lucy Davis.

Patty Jenkins

When Patty Jenkins was seven years old, her father, William T. Jenkins, died after his plane crashed into the ocean during a combat-training exercise—much like Steve Trevor's plane crashed into the ocean around Themyscira. Her father was an Air Force captain and fighter pilot who received the Silver Star in the Vietnam War. Her mother, Emily Roth, was an environmental scientist.

Jenkins grew up moving from one air base to another. When her dad died, she moved to San Francisco, California, with her feminist mother and two sisters. That was something she had in common with Wonder Woman—growing up among females. Jenkins fell in love with movies and was first influenced by a superhero's story after watching the 1978 film *Superman* featuring Christopher Reeve. "I remember everything about the experience of seeing it," Jenkins said. "It really hit me in that way of exactly what I think superheroes were designed to do—to inspire you to metaphorically imagine the superhero within."[1]

Jenkins directed her first big motion picture, *Monster*, in 2003. She also directed a few TV episodes. For *Wonder Woman*, the studio first went with *Game of Thrones* director Michelle MacLaren before offering the job to Jenkins. "I always thought, because of 'Superman,' one day I want to make a movie that makes other people feel like that movie made me feel," Jenkins said. "The fact that that's come true is so stunning."[2]

While negotiating her contract, Jenkins made sure to push for being paid what her male equivalent would have been paid. According to many studies, women earn only about 80 cents to every dollar that men receive. "She is definitely paving the way for so many other female directors," Gadot said. "I think it was very important that she fought to get the best deal."[3]

Jenkins became the first female director to direct a superhero film and the first woman to direct a movie with a budget over $150 million. She earned $1 million for directing *Wonder Woman*. She is set to earn $9 million to direct *Wonder Woman 1984*, which will make her the highest paid female director in history.

Patty Jenkins will become the highest paid female director in history for *Wonder Woman 1984*.

1. Quoted in Ramin Setoodeh, "'Wonder Woman' Director Patty Jenkins on Equal Pay, Hollywood Sexism and James Cameron's Nasty Words," *Variety*, accessed on December 27, 2018. variety.com/2017/film/features/patty-jenkins-wonder-woman-hollywood-sexism-equal-pay-james-cameron-1202583237/.

2. Quoted in Setoodeh, "'Wonder Woman' Director Patty Jenkins on Equal Pay, Hollywood Sexism and James Cameron's Nasty Words."

3. Quoted in Setoodeh, "'Wonder Woman' Director Patty Jenkins on Equal Pay, Hollywood Sexism and James Cameron's Nasty Words."

After seeing Diana in action, the men realize that she is right—and they follow her. It is a scene that represents all that the character of Wonder Woman is. She is a fighter, but she is a protector too, and she will take chances to save people. She will do what needs to be done even if other people will not. She is a leader of men and women. Gadot showed all of this in a scene that caused many women to become emotional upon seeing her depict the kind of heroic moment often given only to men.

Gadot believed this moment—and the film in general—resonated with so many people because it was about universal themes and values that all people—men and women—can relate to. "We went back to simple values ... that are very valuable and relevant, especially nowadays," Gadot said. "If it's love and compassion and acceptance and justice, truth, and peace, I hope that this movie will make people look inside and be better, be good."[52]

While Diana and Steve are on the same side during the film, they often clash, as they both have their own ideas of how to defeat evil and end the war. They both come from different backgrounds and have different views about life and morality. Gadot had this to say about Wonder Woman's differences with Steve Trevor:

> Both of them in their core are very good, so they have a lot in common, but on the other hand I think that ... when I start my journey I'm this young idealist who believes that the world is good and mankind [is] good. ... I don't understand the complexities of life and he's the one to educate me and to teach me about the complexities of mankind. And I think she's the one to remind him ... about love, hope, and eventually they have this mutual journey, in which they learn from each other.[53]

Diana believes that if she just kills Ares, she will stop the war, but as the story goes on, she learns that it is not that simple. She makes the wrong decision about which leader is Ares and is stunned when killing him does not stop the war. She is horrified to realize that it is not just Ares who is causing the war, that people do bad things for other reasons, too, and her faith in humanity is shaken. Steve tries to get her to come with him to stop the war, but Diana is upset. She tells Steve that the people do not deserve their help. Steve responds with, "It's not about deserve! Maybe we don't! But it's not about that. It's about what you believe. ... You don't think I wish I could tell you that it was one bad guy to blame? It's not. We're all to blame."[54]

Still, in the end, Diana chooses love, learns something important about herself, and defeats Ares—though not without a major loss.

Jenkins explained how in *Wonder Woman*, the victory is not as evident as in some superhero films:

> *So often superhero victories are obvious. There's a bad guy. He's going to kill people. OK, fine… It was much more symbolic of "I say no to what you all are doing, how you all are living your life. I still love you. I'm still engaged with you. I still understand it's complicated. But I say no to this. To shooting people from afar who you cannot see, I say no."*[55]

A Perfect Fit

In *Wonder Woman*, Diana is developing into the superhero she was meant to become. However, she has a lot to learn in order to get there. This mirrored Gadot's own life in many ways, as she grew up unsure of where her life was heading at first. Still, she was always strong and motivated in whatever she was pursuing. What made Diana stand out from other superheroes in movies was her warmth and her honest displays of emotion, which many people close to Gadot believe are qualities she naturally brought to the role in a way no one else could.

Pine described why he thought Gadot was the best person to play Wonder Woman in the film:

I think the beauty of what Gal has is that she is physically very imposing. She's stunning; she's like six feet tall. She's super strong emotionally and her presence is very captivating. But she also, at the same time, has this beautiful spirit to her that's very ... open and warm and inviting. She's got a wonderful maternal quality to her and a deep kind of love for the world. That is very much this juxtaposition of Diana and Wonder Woman in this film.[56]

Jenkins did not get a say in choosing the actress who played Wonder Woman in the film she was directing. However, when she found out it was Gadot, she was relieved. "They couldn't have found anybody better in the whole wide world," Jenkins said. "Just look at Gal Gadot when she smiles or when she meets somebody and shakes their hand. That is the embodiment of Wonder Woman. She is so beautiful and powerful, but kind and generous and thoughtful. She's just an amazing person."[57]

Triumph of Wonder Woman

Wonder Woman opened June 2, 2017, in the United States. The film set many box office records at the time, making more than $820 million worldwide. The American Film Institute named it one of the top 10 movies of the year.

For a long time, some people were not convinced Wonder Woman could carry her own superhero film. They were unsure how to portray a superhero who represented love and who was not struggling with some other personal internal conflict. Some people also said it would be an issue to make her a likeable and interesting character without objectifying her.

The answer to these problems was (and is) by making her into a multidimensional hero just like any other superhero.

Many female superheroes are often one-dimensional "out of fear that adding any other dimension makes them weak,"[58] Jenkins said. However, Jenkins showed Wonder Woman's strength while allowing Diana's other qualities—her naiveté, growth, and desires—to shine through as well. She proved that Wonder Woman—or any female superhero—could be multifaceted and win the hearts of audiences worldwide. "That's the challenge—how to tell a story of a woman and make it universal," Gadot said. "We are all used to having male protagonists in movies [directed by men]. But the way Patty has captured the Wonder Woman character, she is very relatable to everyone. Boy, girl, man, woman—everyone can relate to her."[59]

Originally, the Wonder Woman of the comics was meant to symbolize female empowerment and the strength of women. However, her representation went through several changes over the years and moved away from that intended symbolism. Jenkins's film returned the story of Wonder Woman back to her original meaning with the help of Gadot, who would play her in at least two other films as well—*Justice League* and *Wonder Woman 1984*.

Chapter Five

Dealing with Life, Fame, and Future Opportunities

The amount of fame Gadot earned from starring in *Wonder Woman* was overwhelming for her at first, but she learned to take it as it came and to be grateful for all the opportunities she had been offered in her career. From there, she would receive many more film project offers. She was now such a well-known actress that she had more options to choose from. She could pick roles with which she felt a real connection, instead of just taking any movie deal that was offered.

While Gadot's acting career was growing, she also had plans to expand her family. She knew this might be tougher because she had committed to starring in multiple films as Wonder Woman. However, she did not let this deter her from focusing on her family life. She was able to balance her family and her career as an actress.

Wonder Woman and Feminism

When people were asking Gadot questions about the *Wonder Woman* film, one thing they often wanted to know more about were her thoughts on feminism.

"People always ask me, 'Are you a feminist?'" Gadot said. "And I find the question surprising, because I think, 'Yes, of course. Every woman, every man, everyone should be a feminist. Because whoever is not a feminist is a sexist.'"[60]

After Gadot landed the role of Wonder Woman, she decided she wanted to play more strong female roles. She wanted to set a good example for her children and show them that a female character does not always have to be reliant on a male character in every story. Her goals now include bringing more substance to female roles, continuing to pave the way in diversifying roles for women in Hollywood, and showcasing feminism in a positive light.

"There are such misconceptions as to what a feminist is," Gadot said. "Feminism is about equality. I want *all* people to have the same opportunities and to get the same salaries for the same jobs. I realize I'm doing what I want to do because of the women before me who laid the groundwork. Without them I wouldn't be an educated working mother who is following her dreams; I wouldn't be here."[61]

While watching a battle scene in *Wonder Woman* during which the Amazons are fighting alongside each other, Gadot commented on how it made her emotional. "It was the first time for me—as a woman, a girl, a female—that I saw an image of strong women that are beautiful and confident and can take care of themselves," she said. "I was shocked by it, and then I was more shocked by the fact that I never saw anything like that."[62]

She realized that the more people experience seeing examples of strong female heroes on screen, the easier it will be for people to understand and accept that both men and women can be the heroes in film, stories, and life in general.

Second Pregnancy

When Gadot and her husband decided to have another child, she didn't let that stop her from working while pregnant on the set of *Wonder Woman* and *Justice League*. When it came time for reshoots for *Wonder Woman*, Gadot was five months pregnant. She did not tell anyone that she had become pregnant during the major part of filming because she did not want to be treated differently than any of the other actors on set.

To disguise her pregnancy on camera during reshoots, the VFX department cut a triangle in the front of Gadot's costume and filled it with green-screen cloth, which they replaced with a flat stomach in post-production to hide her pregnant belly.

"On close-up I looked very much like Wonder Woman," Gadot said. "On wide shots I looked very funny, like Wonder Woman pregnant with Kermit the Frog."[63]

In March 2017, Gadot gave birth to her daughter Maya, her second child. She later posted a photo on social media of herself leaving the hospital with her husband and older daughter, Alma. Alma was pushing newborn Maya in a carrier with balloons attached to it. The caption with the photo read, "And then we were four ... She is here, Maya. I feel so complete blessed and thankful for all the Wonders in my life #family #newborn #grateful."[64]

Speaking about the experience of having her second child, Gadot said, "It's cheesy, but I feel like Wonder Woman when I give birth. When you deliver, you feel like you're a god. Like, 'Oh my God, I made this!' The best thing is to become a mother and to give life."[65]

Justice League

The day after she finished shooting *Wonder Woman*, Gadot began filming *Justice League*. This ensemble movie also featured DC superheroes Batman (played by Affleck), Superman (played by Cavill), Aquaman (played by Jason Momoa), Cyborg (played by Ray Fisher), and the Flash (played by Ezra Miller).

Originally Snyder, who directed *Batman v Superman*, was supposed to direct this film as well. Toward the end of filming,

Special Guest Cameos

After the success of *Wonder Woman*, Gadot became one of the most well-known stars in Hollywood. As her popularity increased, she started making cameos in television shows and music videos. She even had the chance to host *Saturday Night Live*.

Gadot's first guest cameo appearance came on the September 30, 2018, episode of *The Simpsons*. She voiced herself on the episode titled "Bart's Not Dead." In the episode, producers offer the Simpsons a movie deal, and Homer and Ned Flanders hold auditions for the movie. They are looking for actors to play each member of the Simpson family. Gadot auditions for the part of Lisa.

On October 7, 2017, Gadot hosted *Saturday Night Live*. She did a bit with Leslie Jones, who wore a Wonder Woman outfit. Gadot was also featured in a sketch in which she played the role of Diana, otherwise known as Wonder Woman, in her homeland of Themyscira. Her episode was the first one to be broadcast live in Israel.

Gadot was also featured in Maroon 5's music video for their song "Girls Like You," featuring Cardi B. When she appears in the video, she is seen dancing behind singer Adam Levine. The video showcased female celebrities or well-known women who continue to make a positive difference in the world.

however, he dropped out of the director role to spend more time with his family after the loss of his daughter. Joss Whedon, who directed the Marvel Cinematic Universe films *The Avengers* in 2012 and *Avengers: Age of Ultron* in

Gadot attended several events to promote *Justice League* with her costars, from left, Jason Momoa, Henry Cavill, Ezra Miller, Ray Fisher, and Ben Affleck.

2015, stepped in to finish the film. The film was released on November 17, 2017.

In this film, Batman enlists Diana to help him form a group of superheroes to save the world from destruction from the villain Steppenwolf. The team, full of very different characters, has to learn to work together to defeat him.

Gadot explained Wonder Woman's role in *Justice League*: "I think that one of the special things that Diana has … [is] the fact that she just cares for people … in the most sincere way. So when I got the script I made a point out of the importance of Diana being this glue to the team. That she would make each and every one of them, even if it's in small moments, feel stronger and loved and capable."[66]

When asked about her favorite other character out of the *Justice League*, Gadot said it was the Flash: "He's so open and he's very funny. And he's also very vulnerable, like he doesn't come as the guy who's like 'I'm tough. I can fight.' … He's like, 'I've never done this before.' … I appreciate that. Honesty … But I love all of them. I think all of them are great."[67]

While *Justice League* was a long-awaited movie, the audience numbers were largely disappointing. Warner Bros. invested about $300 million in the movie, making it one of the most expensive films ever. The opening weekend for the movie generated only $94 million, and it grossed $657 million worldwide. This made it the DCEU's lowest-grossing film. In comparison, 2012's *Avengers*, Marvel's equivalent of this type of superhero group film, made $207 million its opening weekend and grossed $1.5 billion worldwide, making it one of the highest-grossing films of all time.

Receiving Recognition

Gadot received a lot of recognition for playing the role of Wonder Woman in *Batman v Superman: Dawn of Justice*, *Wonder Woman*, and *Justice League*. However, it was *Wonder Woman* that earned the most awards out of the three films.

Some of the awards the film won in 2018 included Best Action Movie at the Critics' Choice Awards, Best Science Fiction or Fantasy Movie at the Dragon Awards, Best Sci-Fi/Fantasy at the Empire Awards, Outstanding Performance by a Stunt Ensemble in a Motion Picture at the Screen Actors Guild Awards, and Best Female Action Hero from the Women Film Critics Circle, among others. Some of the other unique awards the movie won include Best Fight at the MTV Movie & TV Awards (referring to "Gal Gadot vs. German Soldiers"), and a special Spotlight Award for *Wonder Woman*, Patty Jenkins, and Gal Gadot from the National Board of Review. The movie also won three Teen Choice Awards, including Choice Movie: Action, Choice Movie Actor: Action for Pine's performance, and Choice Movie Actress: Action for Gadot's performance.

Gadot also took home several awards for her role specifically as Wonder Woman, such as the Rising Star Award–Actress from the Palm Springs International Film Festival, the Virtuosos Award from the Santa Barbara Film Festival, and the Best Actress Award at the Saturn Awards. At the Critics' Choice Awards, Jenkins also presented Gadot with the #SeeHer Award, which had only been given out once before, to Viola Davis in 2017. The #SeeHer Award acknowledges outstanding female roles that highlight more accurate portrayals of women in film and television. During her acceptance speech, Gadot explained why the role of Wonder Woman was the role she had always been looking for:

> *Throughout my career I was always asked to describe my dream role and it was clear to me that I wanted to portray a strong and independent woman—a real one—and all of these qualities I looked for I found in her. She's full of heart, strength, compassion, and forgiveness. She commands the attention of the world, and in doing so she sets a positive example for humanity. I want to share this award with all the women and men who stand for what's right, standing for those who can't stand or speak for themselves.*[68]

Gadot was also included on the TIME 100: The Most Influential People of 2018 list. Lynda Carter, who played Wonder Woman in the 1970s TV series, wrote an excerpt for *TIME* magazine praising Gadot for her portrayal of the iconic superhero:

Gadot and Jenkins took home prizes at the 2018 Critics' Choice Awards.

Gal Gadot brought Wonder Woman to millions of new fans. Her portrayal was magnificent and powerful, capturing everything that Wonder Woman represents.

She and I are lucky to be members of this small sisterhood, living and breathing this uniquely strong, smart and charming superhero. I know that as a person, Gal embodies all of these traits. She is a wife and mother; she has served her country, traveled the world, and is hardworking, loving, wise, goofy and full of humanity.

Wonder Woman has helped transform how women and girls see themselves since she emerged on a TV show in 1975. She represents what we know is inside every one of us: fierce strength, a kind heart and incredible valor. Gal understood and captured the spirit of this complex, independent, fully feminine persona. I applaud her for all of her success.[69]

While the film was praised by many, Jenkins did not receive much recognition in the form of awards or nominations. She spoke on this observation with *Entertainment Tonight*: "It's been a little glaring that women directors don't get nominated so often and it is odd particularly when their films are being celebrated in every other way."[70] Gadot also expressed her sentiments about female-directed movies: "I think that having movies that are female led is not charity work. ... It proves itself in the box office and we are 50 percent of the world, so why wouldn't we have 50 percent of ... movie[s] female led,"[71] she said.

Ralph Breaks the Internet

After *Justice League*, Gadot starred in her first animated movie, *Ralph Breaks the Internet*, the sequel to 2012's *Wreck-It Ralph*.

Here, Gadot stands alongside her costars John C. Reilly and Sarah Silverman at the premiere of *Ralph Breaks the Internet*.

She voiced the role of street racer Shank, who helps guide the character Vanellope, voiced by Sarah Silverman. The film follows Vanellope and her best friend Ralph, voiced by John C. Reilly, as they discover a Wi-Fi router in their arcade that transports them to the world of the Internet.

Gadot spoke about what the film offers: "It's all about stories that we ... can all relate to and the balance between ... the humor and also having ... great lessons for all of us to learn from and good reminders about life and friendship."[72]

She also said she really wanted to do the movie because she could not wait to watch it with her daughter: "I just imagined going to the premiere and taking my girl with me and watching this movie together. After reading the script and seeing how amazing the message of this movie is, I really wanted to ... bring this out there to the world."[73]

The movie grossed more than $350 million worldwide. Gadot also accomplished another first in this movie and made her singing debut. She sang the duet "A Place Called Slaughter Race" with Silverman. Since this milestone, Gadot has said she would be open to starring in a musical.

Wonder Woman 1984

Gadot will also play Wonder Woman in the film *Wonder Woman 1984*, to be released on June 5, 2020. The film will be set in the 1980s during the Cold War, and Wonder Woman will be facing off against the classic villain Cheetah, played by Kristen Wiig. Another newcomer to this film is Pedro Pascal. Some fans on Twitter have predicted he will play the role of supervillain Maxwell Lord or Vandal Savage, though as of spring 2019, his role was still unknown.

Other returning characters from *Wonder Woman* include Chris Pine as Steve Trevor, Connie Nielsen as Hippolyta, and Robin Wright as Antiope, meaning some of the characters who died in *Wonder Woman* will return for *Wonder Woman 1984*; although the ways in which they are returning has been a closely guarded secret. Gadot explained that this is a different film from the first one: "The way we all look at it is, it's

Chris Pine and Gal Gadot attended San Diego Comic-Con in July 2018 and answered questions about *Wonder Woman 1984*. They were accompanied by Patty Jenkins, who is joining them once again to direct the film.

not a sequel. It's its own story. It's a different chapter. It's a whole new movie."[74] Jenkins, who will be returning to direct the film, is set to make a record $9 million.

Rumors about the movie include the possibility that Lynda Carter, the actress who portrayed Wonder Woman in the 1970s TV series, may make a cameo in the film. Some fans are speculating that the movie may have to do with George Orwell's dystopian novel *1984*.

At one point, Gadot said she would not return for *Wonder Woman 1984* if Brett Ratner, a producer associated with Warner Bros., received any money from it. Several women had come forward with sexual misconduct allegations against Ratner. However, Ratner's deal with Warner Bros. ended in 2018, and Gadot signed back on for the film.

Gadot announced on December 23, 2018, that the filming for the movie had wrapped. In an Instagram post, she congratulated everyone involved in the making of the movie, including Jenkins, crew members, and others:

We did it. Again!! And as much as the first time shooting Wonder Woman *was amazing, this time was even more unique and special. We shot in 4 very different locations in 3 countries, and I'm so soooo proud of the almost 1000 crew members who came to set every day, giving everything they have into our movie.*

Couldn't ask for better partners on this. I'm so lucky to have the one and only Patty Jenkins, as my director. She always has our backs, she gives us the wings to dare, and everyday she helped us find the most creative version of ourselves. I am so grateful to call her my friend. And to our AMAZINGly talented cast who made every day enjoyable and fun, thank you!

Honestly … Words cannot describe this experience. This journey was so demanding and challenging but we all came

Giving Back

Gadot has made it a priority to give back and participate in charitable organizations. One of these organizations is the nonprofit Pencils of Promise. The group works to brings education to children who are living in poverty all over the world. Gadot said that she is passionate about helping everyone receive an equal chance at happiness and success. In early 2016, she took part in a campaign to raise $35,000 to go toward building a new school. Gadot has also shown support for N:Philanthropy, a fashion company that gives a portion of its proceeds to pediatric cancer research.

In July 2018, Gadot made an appearance at Inova Children's Hospital in Falls Church, Virginia. She wore her full Wonder Woman costume and spent time with children and their families taking photographs. Dr. Lucas Colazzo, a cardiac surgeon, later thanked her for giving her time as he tweeted, "Thank you @GalGadot for visiting us @InovaHealth Children's Hospital. You are a true Wonder Woman. The kids loved it...and so did the staff."[1]

Other causes Gadot has spoken out about are campaigns against domestic violence and sexual assault and misconduct. The actress often uses her social media accounts to speak about these issues.

1. Quoted in Jeff Nelson, "Gal Gadot Makes Surprise Visit to Va. Children's Hospital Dressed as Wonder Woman," *People*, July 8, 2018. people.com/movies/gal-gadot-visits-childrens-hospital-wonder-woman/.

and did our very best every take, every day, putting our all out there and I'm so proud... Thank you universe for this opportunity. I love this character. And thank you to all of you for being the best fans in the world. It was you that made me push myself every day.

I'm so happy and excited, can't wait to share it with you in 2020! ♥ *Gal*[75]

According to Gloria Steinem, one of the leaders of the American feminist movement in the late 1960s and early 1970s, "Wonder Woman's legacy is what we make it. She gave us an idea of justice and compassion and friendship among women, and now it depends on what we do with it."[76] With Wonder Woman's legacy in the hands of Jenkins and Gadot, it seems they will do the character justice.

Wonder Woman: UN Ambassador

On October 21, 2016, Gadot and Lynda Carter were invited to an event at the United Nations (UN) headquarters to celebrate as the Wonder Woman character was named a UN honorary ambassador for the empowerment of women and girls.

"Wonder Woman seeks to promote strength, wisdom, leadership, justice and love," Gadot said to the United Nations. "Qualities that combined make us the very best that we can be. Sometimes we need something or someone to inspire us … a character like Wonder Woman or a real live superhero in your own world."[77] However, some UN staff members and women's rights groups saw no merit in the choice, which caused widespread criticism. A petition was started by "concerned United Nations staff members,"[78] asking for Wonder Woman to be dropped as the UN honorary ambassador. Less than two months later, Wonder Woman lost her title as honorary ambassador.

When Gadot heard the news, she addressed the situation in a profile in *TIME* magazine, noting the fact that Wonder Woman as a symbol is the least pressing issue concerning women in this day and age: "There are so many horrible things that are going on in the world and this is what you're protesting, seriously?"[79]

She also mentioned how women should not be judged on their intellect based upon what they are wearing: "When people argue that Wonder Woman should 'cover up,' I don't quite get it. They say, 'If she's smart and strong, she can't also be sexy.' That's not fair. Why can't she be all of the above?"[80]

Upcoming Film Projects

Gadot has been working on many other films in addition to her latest turn as Wonder Woman, including *Death on the Nile*, an adaptation of a 1937 Agatha Christie story. The movie was directed by Kenneth Branagh. Branagh directed and starred as detective Hercule Poirot in November 2017's *Murder on the Orient Express*, which is based on another one of Christie's tales. *Death on the Nile* follows Poirot as he investigates a murder on a luxurious cruise on the Nile River. Gadot plays the role of Linnet Ridgeway Doyle, a rich heiress who falls in love with Simon, played by Armie Hammer. *Death on the Nile* is set to be released in theaters on December 20, 2019.

Gadot will also star alongside Dwayne Johnson in the action-comedy *Red Notice*, which has a tentative release date of June 12, 2020. The film, directed by Rawson Marshall Thurber, sees Johnson playing the role of an Interpol agent with the mission of capturing the most-wanted art thief in the world. As of spring 2019, more details about Gadot's character have not been revealed yet.

Producing Movies

Gadot is also set to produce her first film, titled *My Dearest Fidel*. The film is about American TV journalist Lisa Howard, who interviewed Cuban leader Fidel Castro in the 1960s. Howard was the liaison between Castro and the White House after the Cuban missile crisis. The film will be based off Peter Kornbluh's *Politico* article, "My Dearest Fidel: An ABC Journalist's Secret Liaison with Fidel Castro." Warner Bros. has acquired the film rights for Sue Kroll, who founded the production company Kroll & Co. Entertainment in April 2018.

THINK OF ALL THE WONDERS WE CAN DO

STAND UP FOR THE EMPOWERMENT OF WOMEN AND GIRLS EVERYWHERE

Lynda Carter and Gadot posed for a photo at the Wonder Woman UN Ambassador Ceremony in 2016. That year marked the character's 75th anniversary.

Kroll will produce the film alongside Gadot and her husband. Gadot may also be playing the role of Howard in the film, although as of spring 2019, that had not been confirmed.

"When I first read Peter's article, I was entranced by his thrilling account of a complicated, fascinating woman in the midst of a high-stakes, real-life drama," Gadot said. "I knew immediately that I had to be involved creatively with telling Lisa Howard's story, and am thrilled to be producing this film with Sue."[81]

The Future Is Female

Since starting her career as an actress, Gal Gadot has portrayed a number of strong and independent women, and she has plans to play more roles just like these. In the beginning, Gadot doubted her abilities, but once she found her footing and became comfortable with the filmmaking industry, she excelled.

"Nothing I planned happened," Gadot said. "But whenever opportunity arose, I was prepared and positive. And all those things I didn't get, all those 'almosts'—if I got them, I wouldn't be Wonder Woman. What's mine is mine, and what's not mine was never meant to be."[82]

Everything she learned—from dancing, serving in the IDF, appearing in beauty pageants, and studying in law school—Gadot later used to help achieve her dreams of becoming an actress. Her coordination and strength training from dancing and combat training helped prepare her for physically demanding roles, such as those in the *Fast and the Furious* films and *Wonder Woman*. The intellect and charisma she honed during her time in beauty pageants and law school made her personable, intelligent, and easy to work with. She used her confidence and assertiveness as a woman in the film industry, demanding what she deserved for her work.

Gadot plans to portray many more strong women in films and showcase their fascinating stories. Some people thought a female superhero could never be a successful movie lead, and she proved them wrong as she dominated the box office and claimed the hearts of many fans.

Gadot is determined to promote feminism and equality in the film industry, including equal pay and opportunities for men and women. "My promise and commitment to all of you is that I will never be silenced, and we will continue [to] band together to make strides, uniting for equality,"[83] she said. There is a lot in store for Gadot's future, and her fans are eagerly waiting to see what she does next.

Notes

Introduction: A Woman Destined to Empower

1. Quoted in Scott Feinberg, "'Awards Chatter' Podcast— Gal Gadot ('Wonder Woman')," *The Hollywood Reporter*, September 6, 2017. www.hollywoodreporter.com/ race-chatter-podcast-gal-gadot-wonder-woman-1035688.

2. Quoted in Feinberg, "'Awards Chatter' Podcast—Gal Gadot ('Wonder Woman')."

Chapter One: Growing Up in Israel

3. "Gal Gadot: Before They Were Famous—Wonder Woman," YouTube video, 7:10, posted by Michael McCrudden, June 8, 2017. www.youtube.com/watch?v=fdkLrXotLTQ&t=99s.

4. Quoted in "Between the Sheets with Model Israeli," TotallyJewish.com, June 2, 2011. web.archive.org/ web/20131212075857/http://www.totallyjewish.com/ entertainment/features_and_reviews/?content_id=16371.

5. Quoted in Alex Morris, "Gal Gadot on Becoming Wonder Woman, the Biggest Action Hero of the Year," *Rolling Stone*, August 24, 2017. www.rollingstone.com/movies/movie-features/gal-gadot-on-becoming-wonder-woman-the-biggest-action-hero-of-the-year-113568/.

6. Quoted in Allison Glock, "The Conversation: Actor, Mother and Superhero Gal Gadot," ESPN, May 30, 2017. www. espn.com/espnw/culture/article/19496814/actor-mother-superhero-gal-gadot.

7. "How Gal Gadot Went From Israeli Army to Miss Universe to Wonder Woman/Screen Tests/W Magazine," YouTube video, 4:07, posted by *W* magazine, April 12, 2017. www.youtube.com/watch?v=ituTGKo986A.

8. Quoted in *Glamour,* "Gal Gadot Is Wonder Woman: 'She Is Not Relying on a Man, and She's Not There Because of a Love Story,'" *Glamour*, March 7, 2016. www.glamour.com/story/gal-gadot-wonder-woman-cover-interview.

9. Quoted in Allison Glock, "No Small Wonder: Gal Gadot Takes Summer by Storm," *Marie Claire*, May 8, 2017. www.marieclaire.com/celebrity/a26979/gal-gadot-june-2017-cover/.

10. Quoted in Morris, "Gal Gadot on Becoming Wonder Woman, the Biggest Action Hero of the Year."

11. Quoted in Chancellor Agard and K. C. Blumm, "From Miss Israel to Wonder Woman: What You Need to Know About Gal Gadot," *People*, June 1, 2017. people.com/movies/gal-gadot-what-to-know-about-wonder-woman-from-batman-v-superman/.

12. Quoted in *Glamour*, "Gal Gadot Is Wonder Woman: 'She Is Not Relying on a Man, and She's Not There Because of a Love Story.'"

13. Quoted in Feinberg, "'Awards Chatter' Podcast—Gal Gadot ('Wonder Woman')."

14. Quoted in Corinne Heller, "Gal Gadot Thought She Was 'Too Smart' to Be an Actress and Could Have Become a Bond Girl," Eonline.com, April 12, 2017. www.eonline.com/news/843021/gal-gadot-thought-she-was-too-smart-to-be-an-actress-and-could-have-become-a-bond-girl.

15. Quoted in Feinberg, "'Awards Chatter' Podcast—Gal Gadot ('Wonder Woman')."

Chapter Two: Speeding Toward Stardom

16. Quoted in *Glamour*, "Gal Gadot Is Wonder Woman: 'She Is Not Relying on a Man, and She's Not There Because of a Love Story.'"

17. Quoted in *Glamour*, "Gal Gadot Is Wonder Woman: 'She Is Not Relying on a Man, and She's Not There Because of a Love Story.'"

18. Quoted in *Glamour*, "Gal Gadot Is Wonder Woman: 'She Is Not Relying on a Man, and She's Not There Because of a Love Story.'"

19. "Fast & Furious 6 Interview—Gal Gadot (2013)—Dwayne Johnson Movie HD," YouTube video, 2:01, posted by Movieclips Coming Soon, May 7, 2013. www.youtube.com/watch?v=ohGDzCykkaU.

20. "Fast & Furious 6 Interview—Gal Gadot (2013)—Dwayne Johnson Movie HD," YouTube video, posted by Movieclips Coming Soon.

21. Quoted in Helen O'Hara, "Paul Walker: How the Fast & Furious Family Said Goodbye," *Telegraph*, April 2, 2015. www.telegraph.co.uk/culture/film/film-news/11492475/fast-furious-7-paul-walker-tribute.html.

22. Quoted in Feinberg, "'Awards Chatter' Podcast—Gal Gadot ('Wonder Woman')."

23. Quoted in Feinberg, "'Awards Chatter' Podcast—Gal Gadot ('Wonder Woman')."

Chapter Three: Becoming Wonder Woman

24. Quoted in Feinberg, "'Awards Chatter' Podcast—Gal Gadot ('Wonder Woman')."

25. Quoted in Feinberg, "'Awards Chatter' Podcast—Gal Gadot ('Wonder Woman')."

26. Quoted in Feinberg, "'Awards Chatter' Podcast—Gal Gadot ('Wonder Woman')."

27. Quoted in Feinberg, "'Awards Chatter' Podcast—Gal Gadot ('Wonder Woman')."

28. Quoted in Feinberg, "'Awards Chatter' Podcast—Gal Gadot ('Wonder Woman')."

29. Quoted in Feinberg, "'Awards Chatter' Podcast—Gal Gadot ('Wonder Woman')."

30. Quoted in Gill Pringle, "Some Kind of Wonderful," Filmink.com.au, January 5, 2016. www.filmink.com.au/some-kind-of-wonderful/.

31. Quoted in Pringle, "Some Kind of Wonderful."

32. Quoted in Feinberg, "'Awards Chatter' Podcast—Gal Gadot ('Wonder Woman')."

33. Quoted in Michele Manelis, "Wonder Woman Gal Gadot Reveals Her Intense Training Regimen," news.com.au, May 29, 2017. www.news.com.au/entertainment/movies/new-movies/wonder-woman-gal-gadot-reveals-her-intense-training-regimen/news-story/4e49a53b444c437f721a72e38c2fe7f9.

34. Quoted in Manelis, "Wonder Woman Gal Gadot Reveals Her Intense Training Regimen."

35. Quoted in Manelis, "Wonder Woman Gal Gadot Reveals Her Intense Training Regimen."

36. Quoted in Alexandra Tunell, "Gal Gadot on Israeli Beauty, Wild Stunts and Wonder Woman Workouts," *Harper's Bazaar*, July 15, 2015. www.harpersbazaar.com/beauty/makeup/interviews/a11526/gal-gadot-beauty-interview/.

37. Quoted in Spencer Perry, "Wonder Woman Will Change How Fans See the Character in Batman v Superman," Comingsoon.net, March 6, 2017. www.comingsoon.net/movies/features/821671-wonder-woman-will-change-how-fans-see-the-character-in-batman-v-superman.

38. Quoted in *Glamour*, "Gal Gadot Is Wonder Woman: 'She Is Not Relying on a Man, and She's Not There Because of a Love Story.'"

39. Quoted in Meredith Woerner, "Gal Gadot Brings Wonder Woman to Life in 'Batman v Superman,'" *Los Angeles Times*, March 24, 2016. www.latimes.com/entertainment/herocomplex/la-et-hc-wonder-woman-gal-gadot-20160324-story.html.

40. A.O. Scott, "Review: 'Batman v Superman' … v Fun?," *New York Times*, March 23, 2016. www.nytimes.com/2016/03/25/movies/review-batman-v-superman-dawn-of-justice-when-super-friends-fight.html?referrer=google_kp.

41. Sandie Angulo Chen, "Batman v Superman: Dawn of Justice," Common Sense Media, March 2016. www.commonsensemedia.org/movie-reviews/batman-v-superman-dawn-of-justice

Chapter Four: A Female Hero

42. "The 'Wonder'ful Gal Gadot," YouTube video, 4:26, posted by TheEllenShow, March 15, 2016. www.youtube.com/watch?v=NTySVAtrdQc.

43. "The 'Wonder'ful Gal Gadot," YouTube video, posted by TheEllenShow.

44. "The 'Wonder'ful Gal Gadot," YouTube video, posted by TheEllenShow.

45. "Wonder Woman Opening Scene/Wonder Woman (2017) Movie Clip," YouTube video, 4:59, posted by Scopian01, September 8, 2017. www.youtube.com/watch?v=iuLbGNieLRY.

46. Quoted in Perry, "Wonder Woman Will Change How Fans See the Character in Batman v Superman."

47. "Wonder Woman (2017)—Diana Discovers Her Power," YouTube video, 2:53, posted by TopMovieClips HD, November 18, 2017. www.youtube.com/watch?v=nQMQb5pZLcE.

48. "Godkiller & Diana's Escape/Wonder Woman [+Subtitles]," YouTube video, 4:51, posted by Flashback FM, October 12, 2017. www.youtube.com/watch?v=qPJHB4EXwgw.

49. "Godkiller & Diana's Escape/Wonder Woman [+Subtitles]," YouTube video, posted by Flashback FM.

50. "Diana & Steve Boat Scene/Wonder Woman (2017) Movie Clip," YouTube video, 4:56, posted by Scopian01, November 4, 2017. www.youtube.com/watch?v=BJDCMz8mRtY.

51. Patty Jenkins, dir. *Wonder Woman*. Burbank, CA: Warner Bros. Home Video, 2017. DVD.

52. "Gal Gadot, Connie Nielsen Chris Pine and Director Patty Jenkins Discuss New Film 'Wonder Woman,'" YouTube video, 30:07, posted by BUILD Series, May 23, 2017. www.youtube.com/watch?v=PZbVpp5hC3A.

53. "Wonder Woman—Gal Gadot & Chris Pine Interview (2017)," YouTube video, 5:38, posted by iHollywoodTV, May 29, 2017. www.youtube.com/watch?v=Z-Xln5BVB4Y.

54. Patty Jenkins, dir. *Wonder Woman*. Burbank, CA: Warner Bros. Home Video, 2017. DVD.

55. Quoted in Belinda Luscombe, "Patty Jenkins: The Director Redefining How the World Sees Women," *TIME*, accessed on December 27, 2018. time.com/time-person-of-the-year-2017-patty-jenkins-runner-up/.

56. Quoted in Ed Gross, "Why Gal Gadot Is the Perfect Wonder Woman (Exclusive)," *Life and Style*, June 2, 2017. www.lifeandstylemag.com/posts/gal-gadot-wonder-woman-133394/.

57. Quoted in Gross, "Why Gal Gadot Is the Perfect Wonder Woman (Exclusive)."

58. Quoted in Luscombe, "Patty Jenkins: The Director Redefining How the World Sees Women."

59. Quoted in Tatiana Siegel, "The Complex Gender Politics of the 'Wonder Woman' Movie," *Hollywood Reporter*, May 31, 2017. www.hollywoodreporter.com/features/complex-gender-politics-wonder-woman-movie-1008259.

Chapter Five: Dealing with Life, Fame, and Future Opportunities

60. Quoted in Morris, "Gal Gadot on Becoming Wonder Woman, the Biggest Action Hero of the Year."

61. Quoted in *Glamour*, "Gal Gadot Is Wonder Woman: 'She Is Not Relying on a Man, and She's Not There Because of a Love Story.'"

62. Quoted in Matthew Mueller, "Gal Gadot Explains Why 'Wonder Woman' Battle Scene Made Her Emotional," Comicbook.com, November 28, 2017. comicbook.com/dc/2017/11/28/gal-gadot-wonder-woman-battle-made-her-emotional/.

63. Quoted in Christopher Hooton, "Wonder Woman: How They Got Around Gal Gadot Being Five Months Pregnant During Reshoots," Independent.co.uk, June 12, 2017. www.independent.co.uk/arts-entertainment/films/news/wonder-woman-gal-gadot-pregnant-filming-vfx-cgi-behind-the-scenes-a7785321.html.

64. Quoted in Dailymail.com Reporter, "'And then we were four!' Wonder Woman Gal Gadot Announces the Birth of Baby Daughter Maya," DailyMail.com, March 20, 2017. www.dailymail.co.uk/tvshowbiz/article-4332776/Wonder-Woman-Gal-Gadot-welcomes-second-daughter.html.

65. Quoted in Manelis, "Wonder Woman Gal Gadot Reveals Her Intense Training Regimen."

66. "Justice League Gal Gadot Wonder Woman Sound Bite Interview," YouTube video, 2:47, posted by Cosmic Book News, November 3, 2017. www.youtube.com/watch?v=mXTEYYQ1cRc.

67. "Gal Gadot Talks Justice League, Wonder Woman & More!," YouTube video, 9:18, posted by KISS FM UK, November 17, 2017. www.youtube.com/watch?v=_tKiBZxuuCw.

68. "Gal Gadot Gives Amazing Speech for the #SeeHer Award at 2018 Critics' Choice Awards: Watch!," YouTube video, 2:09, posted by *Entertainment Tonight*, January 12, 2018. www.youtube.com/watch?v=18GF2vm_1aI.

69. Lynda Carter, "Gal Gadot," *TIME*, accessed on December 30, 2018. time.com/collection/most-influential-people-2018/5217578/gal-gadot/.

70. "Gal Gadot Gives Amazing Speech for the #SeeHer Award at 2018 Critics' Choice Awards: Watch!," YouTube video, posted by *Entertainment Tonight*.

71. "Gal Gadot Gives Amazing Speech for the #SeeHer Award at 2018 Critics' Choice Awards: Watch!," YouTube video, posted by *Entertainment Tonight*.

72. "Gal Gadot on Ralph Breaks the Internet—interview at premiere in London," YouTube video, 1:39, posted by The Upcoming, November 25, 2018. www.youtube.com/watch?v=6ra-L-0hqdA.

73. Quoted in Scott Baumgartner, "Gal Gadot Says She'd 'Love' to Tackle a Musical After Singing in 'Ralph Breaks the Internet' (Exclusive)," *Entertainment Tonight*, November 27, 2018. www.etonline.com/gal-gadot-says-shed-love-to-tackle-a-musical-after-singing-in-ralph-breaks-the-internet-exclusive.

74. Quoted in "Wonder Woman 1984—SDCC panel // Gal Gadot confirms that it's not a sequel / San Diego Comic con," YouTube video, 4:48, posted by AB Network, July 23, 2018. www.youtube.com/watch?v=tSANVL0ylaY.

75. Quoted in Amy Mackelden, "*Wonder Woman 1984* Has Finished Filming, & Gal Gadot Celebrated with New Set Photos," *Harper's Bazaar*, December 27, 2018. www.harpersbazaar.com/culture/film-tv/a25691823/wonder-woman-1984-gal-gadot-new-set-photos-rumors/.

76. "The Untold Story of American Superheroines: Wonder Human—Documentary [HD]," YouTube video, 54:57, posted by Ring Ding, January 22, 2017. www.youtube.com/watch?v=tHPyg367Alc.

77. Quoted in Viva Sarah Press, "Gal Gadot Promotes Strong Women at UN," israel21c.org, October 26, 2016. www.israel21c.org/gal-gadot-promotes-strong-women-at-un/.

78. Alice Ross, "One Less Woman in Politics: Wonder Woman Loses Job as UN Ambassador," *Guardian*, December 13, 2016. www.theguardian.com/world/2016/dec/12/wonder-woman-un-ambassador-gender-equality.

79. Quoted in Jaleesa M. Jones, "Gal Gadot on the Wonder Woman U.N. Backlash: 'This Is What You're Protesting?,'" *USA Today*, December 20, 2016. www.usatoday.com/story/life/entertainthis/2016/12/20/gal-gadot-addresses-wonder-woman-un-controversy/95662742/.

80. Quoted in Jones, "Gal Gadot on the Wonder Woman U.N. Backlash: 'This Is What You're Protesting?'"

81. Quoted in Dave McNary, "Gal Gadot Producing, Possibly Starring in Fidel Castro Journalism Drama," *Variety*, May 23, 2018. variety.com/2018/film/news/gal-gadot-fidel-castro-journalism-movie-1202820636/.

82. Quoted in *Glamour*, "Gal Gadot Is Wonder Woman: 'She Is Not Relying on a Man, and She's Not There Because of a Love Story.'"

83. Quoted in Alyssa Bailey, "Read Gal Gadot's Powerful Critics' Choice Award Speech About Equality and 'Wonder Woman,'" *Elle*, January 12, 2018. www.elle.com/culture/celebrities/a15066851/gal-gadot-critics-choice-seeher-award-speech/.

Gal Gadot Year by Year

1985

Gal Gadot is born on April 30 in Petah Tikva, Israel.

2004

Gadot wins Miss Israel and enters the Miss Universe pageant.

2005

Gadot begins serving in the Israel Defense Forces as a combat instructor.

2007

Gadot studies law and international relations at IDC Herzliya in Israel; she stars in the Israeli TV series *Bubot*.

2007-2008

Gadot auditions for a Bond girl role in *Quantum of Solace*; she marries Israeli real estate developer Yaron Varsano.

2009

Gadot makes a cameo appearance in *Entourage*; she appears as Gisele Yashar in *Fast & Furious*; and she stars in *The Beautiful Life: TBL*.

2010

Gadot appears in the comedy film *Date Night* and action adventure comedy film *Knight and Day*.

2011

Gadot stars in *Fast Five*; she plays the role of Kika in the Israeli TV series *Asfur*; and she gives birth to daughter Alma.

2012

Gadot stars as Yamit Bareli in the Israeli TV series *Kathmandu*.

2013

Gadot stars in *Fast & Furious 6*; she also auditions for and is cast as Wonder Woman.

2014

Gadot stars as Mirit Ben Harush in *Kicking Out Shoshana*.

2016

Gadot stars as Elena Vlaslov in *Triple 9*; she makes her debut as Wonder Woman in *Batman v Superman: Dawn of Justice*; she plays the role of Jill Pope in *Criminal*; and she plays the role of Natalie Jones in *Keeping Up with the Joneses*.

2017

Gadot stars in *Wonder Woman*; she reprises her role as Wonder Woman in *Justice League*; she hosts *Saturday Night Live*; and she gives birth to daughter Maya.

2018

Gadot is featured in Maroon 5's "Girls Like You" video; she is featured in an episode of *The Simpsons*; she voices the role of Shank in *Ralph Breaks the Internet*; she is cast in the role of Linnet Ridgeway Doyle in *Death on the Nile*; she is cast to star in *Red Notice*; and she finishes filming *Wonder Woman 1984*.

For More Information

Books

Cowsill, Alan, Alexander Irvine, Steven Korte, Matthew K. Manning, and Stephen Wiacek. *The DC Comics Encyclopedia: The Definitive Guide to the Characters of the DC Universe*. New York, NY: DK Publishing, 2016.
This book is an encyclopedia of the many superheroes and characters from the DC Comics world.

Duling, Kaitlyn. *Gal Gadot*. Minneapolis, MN: Jump! Inc., 2018.
This book gives an inside look into Gal Gadot's life and career, including her upbringing in Rosh HaAyin, success in the film industry, marriage to Yaron Varsano, and more.

Lepore, Jill. *The Secret History of Wonder Woman*. New York, NY: Vintage Books, 2015.
Wonder Woman's creator William Moulton Marston is discussed in this book, along with the use of history and various themes included in Wonder Woman.

Sherman, Jill. *Gal Gadot: Soldier, Model, Wonder Woman*. Minneapolis, MN: Lerner Publications, 2018.
Gal Gadot's life as an actress, wife, mother, and activist are highlighted in this book.

Simonson, Louise. *DC Comics Covergirls*. New York, NY: Chartwell Books, 2016.
This helpful guide examines the evolution and comprehensive timeline of the female characters and superheroes of DC Comics.

Websites

DC Comics Official Website
(www.dccomics.com/)
Comic book fans can browse this website to find out more about
their favorite superheroes from DC Comics, including Wonder
Woman and Batman.

Gal Gadot Official Website
(www.galgadot.com/)
This website maintained by Gal Gadot includes photos and links
to her social networking sites.

Gal Gadot on Facebook
(www.facebook.com/GalGadot/)
This website is Gal Gadot's official Facebook page, where
she connects with fans and notifies them about her upcoming
film projects.

Gal Gadot on Instagram
(www.instagram.com/gal_gadot)
Gal Gadot's official Instagram page is where she posts personal
photos to share with fans.

Gal Gadot on Twitter
(twitter.com/GalGadot)
Gal Gadot uses her official Twitter page to connect with her
fans through updates on appearances, film news, and other
life events.

Index

Picture Credits

About the Author

Vanessa Oswald is an experienced freelance writer and editor who has written pieces for publications based in New York City and the Western New York area. These include *Resource* magazine, the *Public*, *Auxiliary* magazine, and the *Niagara Gazette*. In her spare time, she enjoys dancing, traveling, reading, snowboarding, and attending live concerts.